IMAGES
*of Scotland*

# AROUND
# MELROSE

The coat of arms granted to the old Melrose Burgh Council.

IMAGES
*of Scotland*

# AROUND
# MELROSE

*Compiled by*
John W. Butcher

TEMPUS

Tempus Publishing Limited
The Mill, Brimscombe Port,
Stroud, Gloucestershire, GL5 2QG

ISBN 0 7524 1159 4

Typesetting and origination by
Tempus Publishing Limited
Printed in Great Britain by
Midway Clark Printing, Wiltshire

A view of Melrose from the 'Turn Again Stone' above Abbotsford by an unknown artist.

# Contents

# Acknowledgements

The Historical Association would like to thank all those who have been involved in the production of this book: John Butcher, who has acted as the general editor; Anne Gordon, Jack Sugden and Peter Wood, each of whom composed captions for various photographs and who provided some postcards and pictures; William Windram, who let some of his postcards be included; George Thomson, who not only helped with the captions but also put all the text onto disk; Historic Scotland, the National Monuments Record of Scotland and W.S. Sellar for allowing images of Melrose Abbey and railway engines to be used. My apologies to any who have been omitted. Finally, special thanks must be given to Tom Little for providing most of the photographs from his own collection and for his invaluable help with all of the captions and text. Without him this book would not have been possible.

The old parish church, which burnt down in 1908.

# Introduction

Melrose means 'the bare promontory', or possibly 'the bare moor/meadow', and was used for the original settlement founded by St Aidan on a promontory on a loop of the River Tweed, two or three miles downstream from the modern town. Eventually the name was transferred to the twelfth-century abbey. However, as Jessie MacDonald writes in *Place-Names of Roxburghshire*, 'the badge of the Cistercians who founded the abbey is a rose, so the mythologians got busy and interpreted the name as "the hammer and the rose", which is depicted on the Melrose coat of arms. In the New Statistical Account of 1834 the parish minister of Melrose, the Revd George Thomson, dubbed it (the coat of arms) "a pun on Melrose".'

Billions of years ago Melrose was formed geologically where the Sahara Desert now is and since then has drifted north to its present position. Three hundred million years ago the three main Eildons were formed as a result of volcanic activity beneath the earth's crust. They are now exposed as hills after millions of years' weathering. The technical name for such intrusion is a composite laccolith. The Little Eildon is the remains of a volcano that erupted 250 million years ago.

In AD 1133 King David I brought twelve Cistercians from Rievaulx to Old Melrose. However, they soon realised that Old Melrose was unsuitable for their abbey sheep farming, so they selected a site in the broad meadows on the south bank of the River Tweed, at the foot of the Eildon Hills. To ensure a constant supply of water to the abbey, the monks constructed the 'Mill Lade' and even managed to divert the course of the Tweed. The end of the abbey came in 1544-5 and many locals used its ruins as a convenient source of stone. The ruined nave was converted into the Parish Church in 1618 and remained in use until 1810.

After the demise of the abbey Melrose continued to grow peacefully and quietly as a thriving market town, with the market square grouped around the market cross. In the nineteenth century Melrose had a sizeable linen industry and a bleach field, but the rapid growth of Galashiels as a manufacturing centre brought the linen industry to an end. Several of the larger houses situated around the town were built for the owners of mills located elsewhere in the Borders. Melrose is now a quiet, unhurried, country community, catering for the farms and rural villages that surround it as well as for the Borders General Hospital. Many visitors and tourists of all nationalities pass through each year, attracted by both the abbey and the Eildons.

## MELROSE HISTORICAL ASSOCIATION

The association was formed in the 1970s under the guidance of the Revd Bob Henderson, the minister of St Cuthbert's parish church, his wife, Margaret Henderson, and other Melrose historians. Its aims were to promote interest in the history of Melrose and district, to record information and to preserve items of interest which were in danger of being lost. The association attempts to achieve these aims by three specific activities. Firstly, there are six meetings during the winter months when lectures are given by members and visiting speakers on a variety of subjects. In 1998-99 these range from 'The Haunted Borders' and 'The Iron Age in the Borders' to 'Queen Victoria's Physician' and '1/4th KOSB after Gallipoli'. Secondly, in the summer months there are visits to local places of interest, with guided tours in and around Melrose. Lastly, members have produced publications which include *Places of Interest around Melrose*, *Melrose 1826*, *A Walk around Melrose*, *Fair Melrose*, and *Melrose, Its Kirk and People*. The Association has also published six bulletins to date and has recorded the field names of the Melrose Parish.

Melrose Abbey in 1814, an engraving by A. Nasmyth.

# One
# Melrose Abbey

*The abbey was one of the most beautiful ecclesiastical buildings of the Middle Ages. Built between 1136 and 1146, it housed the first Cistercian monks in Scotland, who came to Melrose from Rievaulx. Its church was, like all Cistercian churches, dedicated to the Blessed Virgin Mary. The abbey was last flamboyantly rebuilt between 1503 and 1507 and ceased to exist in 1565 when the last monk, Dan John Watson, joined the Reformed Kirk. The nave of the church was used as the parish church from 1618 to 1810. The abbey's ruins still attract tourists and visitors from all over the world.*

Old Melrose from 'Scott's View'. This piece of land, about four miles east of modern Melrose, was the site of the original monastery founded by St Aidan in AD 635-651.

An imaginative drawing by Alan Sorrell of the abbey as it would have appeared in its heyday. The Cistercian monks who came to Old Melrose in 1133 moved to the present site, a gift from King David, in 1136. The abbey was seriously damaged during English invasions in 1322 and 1385 and was finally destroyed in 1545 by the Earl of Hertford during the 'Rough Wooing' of Henry VIII. (Crown Copyright: reproduced by permission of Historic Scotland.)

The Abbey Hotel, seen here at the west end of the abbey, was demolished in 1948 soon after this photograph was taken. The cloisters were on the north side, with the Commendator's house seen just beyond. To the north-west is Harmony Hall (see p. 116).

There are many interesting and historical gravestones in the abbey graveyard. This one commemorates the Covenanter Nichol Cochrane.

A 1761 gravestone with a comment on the futility of human aspirations.

The floor of the chapter house was excavated in 1921. (Crown Copyright: Royal Commission on the Ancient and Historical Monuments of Scotland.)

These graves were excavated at the door of the chapter house, beneath the tomb of St Waltheof, second abbot of the monastery. (Crown Copyright: Royal Commission on the Ancient and Historical Monuments of Scotland.)

This leaden casket was also discovered in the 1921 excavation of the chapter house floor and was found to contain an embalmed human heart. (Crown Copyright: Royal Commission on the Ancient and Historical Monuments of Scotland.)

Tradition identifies this as the embalmed heart of King Robert the Bruce, buried in Melrose Abbey at his special request. Excavated again in 1996, the casket, after careful examination of its contents, was enclosed in a special container and re-interred with reverent ceremony on 22 June 1998. (Crown Copyright: Reproduced by permission of Historic Scotland.)

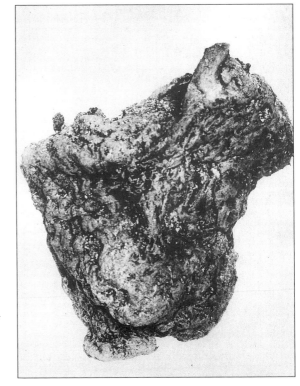

This plaque marked the site where the casket was originally buried. It has now been replaced by a new plaque following the 1998 re-interment.

This view of the abbey, seen from the west, was taken after the demolition of the Abbey Hotel in 1948 (see p. 10).

This carving of a monkish figure, originally in the abbey, has unfortunately long since been removed. It was a late carving, supposedly representing the 'lay of the last minstrel' – 'The Monk of St Mary's Isle'.

Some carvings have survived the ravages of time and vandalism. This one, of a fox and two geese, is high up on the staircase tower and faces north-west into the building.

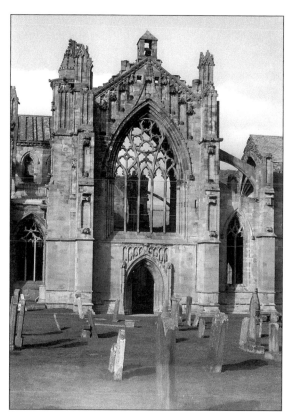

On the south transept gable is the belfry holding the Buryerhuys bell, which was cast in Holland in 1608 by Jan Buryerhuys. A relic of the first Protestant church in Melrose, it summoned the townspeople to worship for over 300 years until 1975.

The Buryerhuys bell is inscribed '*Soli Deo Gloria*' ('To God alone be the glory'). It was restored in 1990 and is now operated electronically, ringing every Sunday at 9 a.m. and 10 a.m.

# Two

# Central Melrose and Schools

*The centre of Melrose is grouped round the market square and market cross. Markets are no longer held here; instead, cars now park where stalls would have been set up and animal sales held. Melrose has its complement of shops, hotels and banks, as well as a post office. The high street runs west from the market square. Off the High Street to the south lie Gibson Park, the caravan site, the old grammar school (founded in 1662, built in 1876, closed in 1990 and now the Teachers' Centre) and the new grammar school, opened in 1990. To the north are the Greenyards, Melrose Rugby Ground and the parish church.*

The Cross is the market cross of the burgh. It probably replaced an earlier one that is known to have stood farther to the north-east, in front of the abbey gatehouse. It is of sixteenth-century type and appears here in its original form, with an octagonal stepped base supporting an octagonal shaft and with a unicorn on top. The houses have thatched roofs. This is an engraving by J. Greig from a painting of L. Clennell in 1814.

In this picture, *c*. 1814, the building behind the Cross is the Black Bull Hotel, with the abbey to the right. The Cross's shaft had a unicorn on top, holding a shield bearing the royal arms. The supporting capital was dated 1645, with a sundial behind, which on one side had a shield showing the mell and rose of Melrose and on the other the initials IEH for John, 4th Earl of Haddington.

A mid-nineteenth-century view towards the Cross shows the developments that have taken place. Although some thatched houses remain, the handsome Burt's Hotel has been built on the right of the picture.

This bustling scene (1840s) shows the Pant Well, a hexagonal building beside the Cross, built in 1839 and used until around 1859. Water was piped from the hills and stored in a tank within the Pant Well as a supply for the townspeople.

A woman drawing water at the Pant Well (1840s). There was also a trough for animals.

The base of the shaft has now been altered, rising from two post-1861 octagonal drums of masonry with a more modern base. This view looks westwards down the high street. Although the roads are still unmade, slates have completely replaced thatch.

At the back of the block of buildings on the right stands the tollhouse at the East Port where market dues were formerly paid. One thatched house remains in this pre-1903 view.

In this view from 1903, the Pant Well has been replaced by a small iron fountain (between the cross and the gas lamp) that was used until the 1930s. The tobacconist's shop is now Russell's Restaurant. Thomas Russell's drapery is now the library but it was once the home of Captain Ormiston on whom Sir Walter Scott based the character Captain Clutterbuck in *The Monastery*. The railway bridge in the background has since been replaced by a bridge for the Melrose bypass road.

The building on the right, built by John Smith of Darnick and photographed in the late nineteenth century, is the only surviving structure of a fire in 1897 that destroyed the rest of the block. A town house was built behind in 1822. The Black Bull Hotel formerly stood where the Bank of Scotland now stands to the left of the Cross. The house and shop to the right are still standing as a shop with flats above.

21

This is James Bunyan's butchers shop, photographed in the early twentieth century, now G.W. Miller, butcher. As time went on, less was sold in the open marketplace and shops such as this soon developed. Melrose is now a good shopping centre for a considerable surrounding district.

A view of modern Melrose. The capital and unicorn of the cross were restored in 1990 and the shaft in 1998. The base is always cheerful with bedding plants in summer.

This view of the East Port was taken in 1990. The seventeenth-century tollhouse was restored in 1981 by the Scottish Special Housing Association in conjunction with the Historic Buildings Council.

The electrician's shop and house between the Ormiston Rooms and Burt's Hotel was demolished in 1973 to provide an entrance to the hotel car park. The house below the hotel is now part of the hotel and the cottage below this house has disappeared.

This photo of the restored market cross in the market square was taken around 1900.

Looking east along the high street towards the market square. The King's Arms and the George and Abbotsford hotels are on the right. Sir Walter Scott used to meet his friends at the George, including James Hogg and, on their visits to Scotland, William and Dorothy Wordsworth.

The Abbey Hotel used to stand in front of the abbey on the west side. It was pulled down in 1948.

The royal party outside the Abbey Hotel on the occasion of the visit by King George V and Queen Mary in 1923.

Burt's Hotel was known as 'Anderson's Temperance Hotel' as late as 1901.

This is Melrose's first fire engine in 1902. The uniforms came later!

This First World War 'tank' was in fact a mock-up, built to raise funds for the war.

The prominent tall building is the present premises of the Bank of Scotland. Also in the picture are a charabanc, milk lorry, bus and cars of the 1920s. On the left, beneath the clock, are a few of the Melrose people of that era.

ROYAL BANK, Melrose.

In 1901 this building was occupied for a short time by the post office. Five members of staff are pictured here. The building as it stood in 1901 was built by Mr Pringle Pattison on the site of a house occupied by Captain Doolittle, who is mentioned in Captain Clutterbuck's 'Introductory Epistle' to *The Monastery*. The Royal Bank moved in after the post office was transferred to Buccleuch Street. The plans for the new premises of the Royal Bank went before the Dean of Guild Court in 1903. There was further refurbishment in the 1970s.

Buccleuch Street. All the Melrose worthies were at the official opening of the new post office in 1901. There were also post office staff, including telegraph boys. There appear to be very few ladies present.

The building on the right is the post office, with the postman standing outside. On the left is Johnston & Aitchison's furniture shop, which is now Marmion's Brasserie. The Congregational chapel is next on the left. It ceased to be used in 1878 and is now a flat and two shops.

The 'marriage ball' is about to be kicked by the bride, Shirley Hastie. The ball will be kicked down the High Street. This custom replaced the original hand ball game.

Contrast this 1997 view with that on p. 27. The white building is the Bon Accord Hotel, which came into being in 1948 after the conversion of the existing house property. The cars show how their design has developed since the 1920s.

This photograph (c. 1900) shows two of the post office staff and three messenger boys with a nineteenth-century bicycle. The office occupied what is now the Royal Bank of Scotland.

Here are the counter staff and postmen who worked at the new post office. (1901)

The school is in the foreground with the parish church of St Cuthbert in the centre and a glimpse of the river Tweed in the distance.

The old Grammar School was replaced by a new school built alongside, opened in 1990.

Mr Thomas Ingram, the Grammar School headmaster, is seen here with a class in around 1900.

A contrasting style of dress is provided by this photograph of a class in the 1960s with their teacher Mrs Nancy Little (whose husband provided much of the material for this book). Mrs Little is on the left with Mrs E. Hunter, the infant mistress, in the centre, and Miss Russell, another primary teacher, on the right.

The old town school, with the schoolmaster's house, stood in Little Fordel before the Grammar School was built.

This is Thomas Murray, who occupied the schoolmaster's house. He was appointed schoolmaster in 1820 and died in 1873.

The inscription that was on the old Grammar School building has now been inset above the entrance doorway of the new school. Its original came from the old Melrose school founded by David Fletcher in 1662.

The new Grammar School was opened in 1990.

Abbey Park, a classical villa built in 1820, has been home to St Mary's Preparatory School for over a century.

The house was built in 1870, possibly as a school since at the beginning of the century there were five ladies from Edinburgh who were boarding there. It ceased to be a school in 1928, and was later called Trinity House. It is now called Riverslea.

# *Three*
# Churches and People

*Melrose has been well endowed with churches. Apart from the abbey, there have been a Methodist church, a Congregational church, which occupied three buildings, an Episcopalian church and three churches of the Church of Scotland. Today only three remain: the parish church on the Weirhill and both Holy Trinity, the Episcopalian church, and High Cross, the Roman Catholic church, in High Cross Avenue. Well-known 'worthies' from Melrose range from Sir Walter Scott, David Brewster, Catherine Helen Spence and Elizabeth Clephane to George Halliburton, the roadman.*

The nave of the abbey was used as the parish church from 1618 to 1810, when the congregation moved to a new church built on the Weirhill. This church stood from 1810 until 1908.

A new church was built and opened in 1911 after the 1810 church building was destroyed by fire in 1908, with only the tower and spire remaining. This church was called St Cuthbert's after its congregation united with the formerly United Free Church congregation of St Aidan's in 1946.

Originally Melrose Free Church, St Aidan's became a congregation of the new United Free Church, formed by the union in 1900 of the Free Church of Scotland with the United Presbyterian Church. By the later union in 1929 of the United Free Church with the Church of Scotland, St Aidan's became a parish church of the Church of Scotland. In 1946 the congregation united with the other parish church in Melrose to form one congregation worshipping in the church called St Cuthbert's.

Nicknamed 'the Kirk in the Garden', the original premises of the United Presbyterian Church were on the upper floor above stables and coach-houses. The congregation moved into a new church in High Cross Avenue in 1866.

High Cross church was built in 1866 to house the congregation who had worshipped previously in 'the kirk in the garden'. It became a United Free Church in 1900, then a parish church in 1929 and finally joined with St Cuthbert's congregation to form Melrose parish church (see p.38) in 1984. The High Cross church building was taken over as a Catholic church, which it remains.

The original Congregational church was built in 1842 and used until 1878.

This Congregational church was built in 1878. It served the local congregation of the Congregational Union until its closure in 1930. Since then it has been a cinema, an antiques business and a coal merchant's. The building is now used by the East of Scotland Water Department.

The Holy Trinity church was designed by Sir George Gilbert Scott and was built in 1849 for the Scottish Episcopal Church.

In 1849, when Catherine Helen Spence was aged fourteen, she and her family, who had lived in Melrose in what is now the Bon Accord Hotel, emigrated to Adelaide, South Australia. Catherine Spence was a noted writer, a champion of orphans and a fighter for women's rights. One of her novels was re-published as recently as 1970 and her face is featured on one of a set of stamps of famous Australian women. She twice revisited Britain and her autobiography has fascinating descriptions of her life as a child in Melrose.

This memorial window to Mrs Anne Ross Cousin (1824-1906) is in the Melrose parish church vestry. Mrs Cousin was the author of the hymn 'The sands of time are sinking'. She was a friend of Elizabeth Clephane (1830-1869), who was known as 'the sweet singer of Melrose' and who wrote the hymns 'Beneath the Cross of Jesus' and, made famous by Moody and Sankey, 'There were ninety and nine that safely lay, In the shelter of the fold'.

These two brass memorial plates were originally erected in St Aidan's church and were brought to Melrose parish church in 1946 at the union of the two congregations.

THE WINDOW ADJACENT IS ERECTED

in Memory of

MRS ANNE ROSS COUSIN

Authoress of "IMMANUEL'S LAND" ('The last words of Samuel Rutherford). and OTHER HYMNS.

Born 27th APRIL, 1824.    Died 6th DECEMBER, 1906.

and Widow of the

REV. WILLIAM COUSIN

Minister of this Church, 1859-1883.

TO THE GLORY OF GOD

AND SACRED TO THE MEMORY OF

ELIZABETH CECILIA DOUGLAS CLEPHANE

Third Daughter of the Late

ANDREW DOUGLAS CLEPHANE (OF CARLOGIE)

Sheriff-Principal of Fife and Kinross

Authoress of the Favourite Hymn

*The Ninety and Nine.*

Born 10th JUNE, 1830.    Died 19th FEBRUARY, 1869.

Mr Jamieson, a Melrose roadman, was a notorious local worthy, known to the children – and others – as 'Jamie Cheuch'. (1900.)

Another local worthy was the bellman Simon Paterson, who was born at the end of the eighteenth century. He was present at George IV's visit to Edinburgh in 1822. He was well known for his cry – 'Now can ye get by?'

This Melrose notable, the roadman George Halliburton, is still remembered for his love of Robert Burns' poetry. He used to recite the poem 'Tam O' Shanter' at Burns suppers.

James Scott, born in the nineteenth century, used to be a blacksmith in Scott's Place and later opened the first garage in Melrose. He was an expert marksman and during the First World War he enlisted and was an Armour Sergeant, becoming a Major later. In Canada, before the war, he won the Palma Trophy for shooting. Palma Place was named after the trophy and the two buildings on the north side of Palma Place were constructed by Scott. He was killed in 1916.

*Four*

# The Greenyards, Rugby and Other Sports

*The name of the Greenyards appears on old maps, but it is now the home of the Melrose Rugby Club. In 1883 Ned Haig invented the knock-out tournament variation of the game, the 'Sevens'. For years Melrose has been invaded by rugby enthusiasts on the second Saturday of April for the annual Melrose Sports or 'Sevens'. In recent years Melrose Rugby XV has been the national champion and has provided players for the Scottish national team. Melrose now has a ladies' rugby team, a hockey team, a cricket club, a fine nine-hole golf course that nestles beneath the Eildons and a bowling green. Curling no longer takes place.*

This photograph shows the Greenyards before it was drained for use as a rugby ground in 1877. St Aidan's church is in the background.

In the background of the Greenyards on a snowy day are two of the Eildon Hills. The picture was taken before the grandstand was erected on the east side of the rugby pitch. Also, there is no terrace on the west side so this picture must date from before the Abbey Hotel was demolished (1948), as the rubble from the hotel formed the foundation of the west terracing.

The gravestone of Ned Haig (1855-1939), the originator of the 'Sevens', is in Wairds Cemetery.

The Sevens Tournament, held in April each year, attracts large numbers of visitors to Melrose (an estimated average of twelve thousand). In this 1983 photograph note the old Grammar School, left of centre, which is now the Teachers' Centre, the allotment square, the white school dining hall and the infant school. The area is now occupied by the new Grammar School.

A try is scored during the second round of the 1990 'Sevens', when Glasgow High/Kelvinside play Edinburgh Academicals. The Greenyards is seen under the Eildons with Newlyn Road and Douglas Road in the background. Some of the large crowd can be seen along with television cameras to the right of the posts.

Melrose playing Randwick in the 1990 'Sevens' Semi-final. Behind the teams is the grandstand with the North Eildon in the background.

Members of Melrose Rugby Club first XV between 1877 and 1883. The horizontal stripes of yellow and black survive today, but the trousers and high boots have long since disappeared.

The last time 'Fastern's E'en Football' was played in the market square was in 1901, before the game was abolished by the town council.

The curling pond used to be at the foot of the Eildon Hills. These are members of the Melrose Curling Club in 1895.

Melrose bowlers enjoy a game. The present bowling green is behind Melrose parish church on the Weirhill.

Melrose Golf Course is at the top of Dingleton Road, nestling at the foot of the Eildons. Here, golfers are shown putting on the first green in 1920. It should be noted that the climb up the Eildon Hills starts from the golf course.

The Melrose Cricket Ground at Huntlyburn, Darnick, in the 1970s. Behind the cricket square is the field in front of Harleyburn Lodge where the Borders General Hospital, opened by the Queen in 1988, was built.

# Five
# The Railway

Melrose lies on the route of the Waverley Line, which ran from Edinburgh through Carlisle to London. Passenger through services between Edinburgh and Hawick commenced on 1 November 1849 and between Hawick and Carlisle on 1 July 1862. From May 1876 Melrose passengers could travel to and from London St Pancras without changing. The last London train, the 21.55 night Midland sleeper service, ran on Saturday 4 January 1969, and was held up at Newcastleton by an organised protest against closing the line. The very last train to run the Waverley line left Edinburgh at 22.20 on 4 January 1969, reaching Hawick after midnight, where its passenger function terminated, and continuing to Carlisle as a parcels train. From the very beginning, Melrose was an important station on the Waverley Line; hence the imposing station buildings that still survive, no longer facing railway tracks but the Melrose bypass.

Melrose in around 1850, looking north from Quarry Hill towards Gattonside Heights and the Black Hill of Earlston in the background. The abbey is central. There is a train of early vintage just leaving the station on its way to Galashiels. It is a single engine and is pulling some antiquated coaches. In the foreground are ladies and children wearing Victorian dress.

Queen Elizabeth and the Duke of Edinburgh having just alighted from the Royal Train at Melrose Station on 5 July 1962. The station master, Tom Little, is being presented to the Queen. Standing on the Queen's right is the Duke of Buccleuch, the Lord Lieutenant of Roxburghshire.

This 1920 view looks east towards Newtown St Boswells, the next station on the line. Both platforms at Melrose Station are wider than average because when the station was constructed in 1849 there were four tracks passing through the station, becoming two tracks at the east end. In 1886 the two-platform tracks were lifted and the platforms extended to the two central tracks.

Melrose Station was renovated in 1986 and this view, taken from the same angle as above, shows the main platform and buildings. The rest of the station has been completely removed and is now occupied by a stretch of the Melrose bypass, opened in 1988. What was the station yard is now a small housing estate, Newlyn Drive.

Melrose Station and the derelict track bed of the railway can be seen here before the bypass was constructed and the station itself was renovated. Behind the station are Gibson Park and the caravan park before being upgraded in 1998. The old Melrose Grammar School can be seen behind Gibson Park.

On 10 July 1921 a goods train came off the rails while passing Darnick. Debris piled up for some distance along the track and barrels of beer were strewn over the line.

The station master, in the centre, is seen here with five of his staff in the 1920s. The sign top left reads 'STATION FOR WAVERLEY HYDROPATHIC', referring to the Waverley Castle Hotel at Darnick (see p. 77).

G. Dalgetty, the station master, is standing in the centre with two porters and two booking-office staff (1940). The iron footbridge linking the two platforms was a prominent feature of the station.

Engine No. 218, Class J38, is standing at Melrose Station waiting to proceed to Galashiels (1890s). The single carriage is one from the old North Eastern Railway Company.

The train departing towards Galashiels is the Saturday-only 11.11 a.m. Hawick-Edinburgh Waverley train (1958). The 4-4-0 engine is pulling only four coaches. In the background are houses in Newlyn Road.

## Six
# Melrose Festival

*The festival was started in 1936. As there were no marches to ride, it was decided that a perambulation of the surrounding countryside and historic places should take place. Since then there have been several changes to the week's festivities. The 'Rideout' takes place on the Monday, a fancy dress parade on the Wednesday and on the Saturday sites connected to the history and heritage of Melrose are visited, on neither foot nor horseback but rather by car and coach. However, there is no longer a visit to Thomas the Rhymer's stone. On the Sunday the Melrosian and the Festival Queen are 'kirked'. Then, on the Thursday, they are 'installed' and 'crowned' respectively in the grounds of Melrose Abbey. The town is decked with bunting for the festival week.*

Melrose Festival lasts for a week each June. Each year a Melrosian is chosen to represent Melrose at all the Border festivals. He is supported by his 'left-hand' and 'right-hand' men. Each Monday of the festival week, a large number of riders take part in the Rideout. Here the riders are crossing the River Tweed at Millmount led by the Melrosian, Stewart Bunyan in 1986.

On Thursday of the festival week, in Melrose Abbey, the Melrosian is installed and the Festival Queen, a girl from Primary Class 7 at Melrose Grammar School, is crowned. In 1980 the Festival Queen was Rosemary Butcher, who is seen here with her attendants. The festival chairman was John Barron. The oration was given by the Chief Constable of Edinburgh and the Borders, whose wife crowned the queen. Behind the queen is Rob Moffat, the Melrosian, with his 'left-hand' and 'right-hand' men.

There is a tour of all the local places of interest on the Saturday morning of the festival week. The first stop is at the site of the Masonic Lodge in Newstead (see pp. 90-92). Here the Melrosian, Rob Moffat, is listening to the head Mason giving details of the history of the Masons in Melrose.

After the Masonic Lodge at Newstead, the Roman Fort at Trimontium is visited. Here, in front of the Trimontium Stone (see p. 87), a 'Roman soldier' reads a proclamation from the occupants of the Roman fort addressed to the Melrosian, the Festival Queen and court and all the followers in 1986.

Gattonside, because of its sunny aspect, used to be the orchard for Melrose Abbey. When the Melrosian, the Festival Queen and their followers arrive at Gattonside they are all given cherries as a reminder of the fruit grown there by the monks.

After Gattonside, the next visit is to Abbotsford, the home of Sir Walter Scott (see pp. 65-70). Here the Melrosian and the queen were greeted by the owners of Abbotsford, the late Mrs Patricia and Dame Jean Maxwell Scott, Sir Walter's great-great-great-granddaughters. The two ladies can be seen in the back row to the left.

The queen and her court can be seen here in the grounds of Darnick Tower, a peel tower. The people of Darnick are allowed access to the garden to welcome the Melrosian and the queen. Darnick Tower is a private residence occupied by Mrs Wilson.

The visits around Melrose finish in Melrose Abbey. The Melrosian, the queen and their followers are greeted by the monks. The charter of King David for the foundation of the abbey is read aloud and the monks can be heard chanting plainsong.

At the conclusion of the ceremonies, the Melrosian and the queen make their way to the place where the heart of King Robert the Bruce is believed to be buried. Here, in 1982, the queen, Morag McKenzie, places her bouquet above the plaque that indicates the burial of the heart.

# Seven
# Abbotsford

In 1811 Sir Walter Scott paid 4,000 guineas for land on the south bank of the Tweed. The land consisted of a haugh called Newharthaugh and a farmhouse and steading called Clarty Hole. The name was changed to Abbotsford because the monks of Melrose had used the ford near the house. The house was enlarged in 1818, the old farm was demolished in 1822 and in 1824 the new buildings were occupied. John Smith of Darnick did some of the work. Sir Walter Scott's granddaughter Charlotte and her husband James Hope-Scott improved the house and grounds. In the mid-1850s a west wing was added to the house which included the chapel. The entrance lodge was built at the same time.

This bust of Sir Walter was completed by Sir Francis Chantrey in 1820. It stands at the east end of the library where it was placed by the young Sir Walter on the day of his father's funeral.

The north side of Abbotsford House, with the River Tweed in the foreground. Abbotsford gets its name from the ford which used to be there in early times. Later the ford was replaced by a ferry, which the maids and servants used to get to and from Galashiels. The ferry ceased to ply during the late 1930s. Now, near the old ford, a road bridge crosses the Tweed. The Galashiels Rideout still crosses the river by the old ford.

Abbotsford House and gardens are seen here from Gala Hill, which is to the north. Originally the little farmhouse and steading was called Clarty Hole. There were two extensions/alterations, the first of which was completed in 1818 by Sanderson and Paterson of Galashiels. This extension was to the east of the old farm house and consisted of an armoury, dining-room, study and conservatory on the ground floor and three bedrooms on the first floor. In 1824 the second alteration was finished by John Smith of Darnick. The farmhouse was demolished and the present main block was built.

This clearly shows the two phases in the completion of Abbotsford House. In this view from the garden court, the block to the right represents the first phase, where all the rooms on the ground floor are now open to the public. The block further back is the second phase and is now the private quarters.

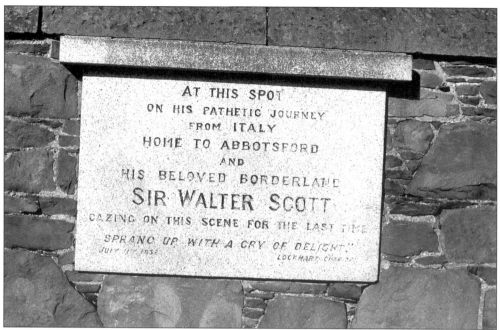

The memorial tablet to Sir Walter Scott is on the Langlee Road in Galashiels. Sir Walter used to join the 'Blucher' at Melrose Bridge tollhouse, which was demolished around 1962. He passed this view journeying to and from Edinburgh. On his last journey from Edinburgh on 1 July 1832, though very ill, he regained consciousness to recognize Abbotsford at this very spot. He died at Abbotsford at 1.30 on 21 September.

This was the view from the memorial tablet in 1946. Note the gasworks on the right, the hayfield in the foreground and the omnipresent Eildons in the background.

The next two pictures were taken at the memorial tablet in 1998. Looking south there is part of Langlee housing estate where the hayfield used to be (see p. 69). The gas holder can still be seen above the house to the right.

This view, looking west from the memorial tablet, shows the modern road bridge that is upstream of the Abbot's Ford, formerly referred to as the Nether Barns Ford. Just above the chimney pot in the centre is Abbotsford House – the view Sir Walter Scott saw on his last journey.

# *Eight*

# Darnick

*Traces of settlements in the area around Darnick can be related to the building of Melrose Abbey during the twelfth century. Dwellings probably existed on the present location of Darnick village long before that period. During the Middle Ages Darnick developed into an important centre with three peel towers. Darnick Tower remains intact, Fishers Tower is now a ruin and nothing remains of the third tower. There was a steady rise of population in the village and by 1881 the census recorded 661 persons living in Darnick and nearby Bridgend. As Darnick was the centre of Scott country, it attracted a considerable tourist trade in Victorian times. To cope with this, the Waverley Hydropathic Hotel was opened in 1871. Darnick has continued to expand, boosted by the opening of the Borders General Hospital in 1988.*

The original tower at Darnick was built around 1425 by the Heiton family. It was partly destroyed in 1545 and rebuilt in 1569. The early tall tower has had various additions, including a two-storey east wing constructed in 1869 by a local builder, Smith of Darnick. Different uses have been made of the building over the years including that of museum, guest house and the present use as a private residence.

Andrew Currie, a Borders sculptor, worked in Darnick from 1859 to the late 1880s. He produced a number of well-known sculptures including Mungo Park in Selkirk, James Hogg at St Mary's Loch, the Bruce Monument at Stirling and figures on the Scott Monument in Edinburgh. Currie's yard is pictured here with Darnick Tower in 1867.

A feature of interest at Darnick Tower is an iron yett which was obtained from Doune Castle near Stirling.

An early twentieth-century view of Darnick Village. Smith Road is on the left and Abbotsford Road on the right. The house in the centre is The Gables, formerly Orchard Cottage. It was built in 1825 by Smith of Darnick and was probably lived in by Thomas Smith, one of the partners.

The hall on the right of the picture was built in 1891 and dedicated to the memory of John Smith (1827-1869) by his wife, Alison. Its function was to 'benefit and advantage the inhabitants of Darnick.' This was achieved in various ways including meetings, religious services, social gatherings and musical performances.

This is Tower Road in 1867, with the walls of Darnick Tower on the left, a thatched cottage on the right and the school (now demolished) in the centre background.

Darnlee, home of the Smith family, was built by John Smith in 1816. This 1867 picture shows the house, situated in woodland, looking similar to the view today.

Looking north along Smith's Road in 1867. The road still follows the same line, but the houses have been rebuilt or extended with an upper floor.

This is the lower end of Smith's Road, looking north, in the same year. The wheelwright's shop (now demolished) is in the centre. A wheelwright is seated outside, working on a wheel resting on a nave stool.

The Hollies, pictured here in 1867, is a two-storey house in the middle of Darnick. The view is similar today, but the iron railings are missing, having been removed for wartime use.

Three workmen outside a thatched cottage in 1867. They are sharpening a long tool or knife on a grindstone.

Two groups pose at the edge of the bowling green, Darnlee, in 1867. There are children's toys on the green itself.

The Waverly Hydropathic Hotel (the 'Hydro') was constructed between 1869 and 1871. It is one of the earliest mass-concrete buildings in Scotland and contained 140 bedrooms, several dining rooms, billiard rooms and a large lecture room.

The Hydro complex covered thirty-eight acres of grounds and included a section of the River Tweed for trout fishing. Over the years the buildings have undergone much change and the present site is smaller than the original, grand, Victorian concept.

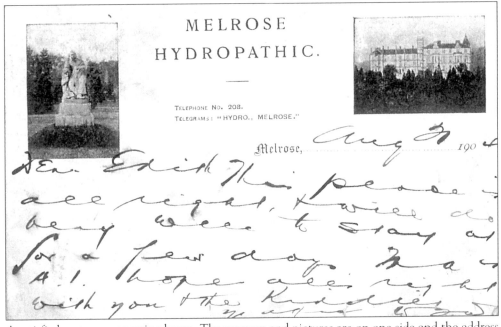

A satisfied customer reporting home. The message and pictures are on one side and the address on the other.

The Hydro can be seen towards the left of the picture rising above the tree line. The house on the riverside towards the right is St Helen's (see p. 79). The scene has changed very little since this photograph was taken in 1905.

This house was built in 1806 for Isaac Haig, a wine trader who retired to the Scottish Borders from the West Indies. It is now privately owned but in the late 1800s was part of the Waverley Hydropathic complex. The grounds contained a well that was famous for its 'pure, sweet, fine water in abundance'.

This appears to be a bust of some unknown person but is in fact a unique sundial designed by John Smith of Darnick in 1830 and located in the garden of St Helen's.

The Elwyn Glen or 'Fairy Dean' was a popular walk along the glen following a series of small bridges. The burn passes under the Galashiels-Melrose road about one mile from Darnick, near the Lowood Bridge where portage was paid. This view shows the glen in 1902.

Pictured here in 1998 is the 'Turn Again Stone'. The Battle of Melrose was fought in 1526 at Skirmish Hill, Darnick. The Scott family and others, who were fighting for the release of James V, were defeated by the forces under Ker of Cessford. Ker led the pursuit, but at the site of the stone Elliott turned and speared Ker to death. The stone was set up to mark the place where Elliott turned again.

This painting of the 'Turn Again Stone' by C. Stanfield shows Melrose in the distance.

To the west of Darnick lies Cauldshiels Loch, about two miles distant. The loch is reputed to be bottomless. In 1941 the ice cream cart and horse of Adam Hall from Galashiels ended up in the loch when the horse went to drink and the weight of the cart pushed them both into the water. The horse drowned and the cart may be still in the loch.

# *Nine*
# Gattonside

*Gattonside lies on the north bank of the Tweed, directly opposite Melrose and its abbey, with which it is connected by a foot suspension bridge. Behind Gattonside rise the low foothills of the Lammermuirs. The monks from the Abbey were quick to exploit the sun-baked, fertile slope of Gattonside for their orchards. Its name is given as Galtunesside (i.e. land belonging to someone called Galtune or Galton) in Melrose's first charter. It is also called Galtuneshauch (i.e. Galtonshaugh) in the same charter. The monks used to cross the Tweed by an 'annay' – a river island – or by an old ford. The ford was used up until eighty years ago for deliveries of coal and large items from Melrose by horse and cart. Last century Sir David Brewster, who invented the kaleidoscope, lived in the house called Allerly.*

This picture shows the main street of Gattonside in 1900. The postman is making his deliveries with his bicycle. Also in the picture is a horse and trap, a popular Victorian form of transport before the advent of the motor car.

*Cherrybank, Gattonside.*

Shown in 1918, this was the home of Adam Dodds, a cabinetmaker, for many years. It is still standing and occupied after being modernised.

Gattonside House was built between 1808 and 1811. It was bought by George C. Bainbridge, a merchant from Liverpool, in 1824. Today it is owned by the Brothers of Charity, an organisation of the Roman Catholic Church, which cares for people with learning difficulties. The chapel that can be seen on the extreme right was built in around 1800 and repaired in 1895. Gattonside House is also now called St Aidan's.

This view, looking north, clearly shows the sunny aspect of Gattonside.

The approach to the chain bridge from Gattonside now has hedges on both sides and the bridge itself looks very different after its refurbishment (see p. 100).

# Ten
# Newstead and Trimontium

*Newstead has often been called the oldest inhabited village in Scotland. There may well have been a settlement here before the Romans established their fort at Trimontium. After the Romans had withdrawn, the civilians almost certainly continued to stay around the now deserted fort. Little is known about Newstead until the first building of Melrose Abbey. As a result of the influx of architects and artisans, some masons may have settled in Newstead. The exact date of the first Masonic Lodge in St John's Wynd is unknown, but in 1675 there were eighty signatures of Masons and employees to the 'mutual agreement' concerning the years of apprenticeship, which were increased from four to seven. After straddling the busy road from Melrose to the A68 and Earlston for many years, Newstead is once again a peaceful village since the opening of the bypass.*

On the east side of Newstead lay the Roman camp of Trimontium, named after the three peaks of the Eildon Hills. The site is marked by this monument, set up in 1928 and renovated in 1997.

This picture shows the ceremony at the unveiling of the restored monument on 30 August 1997 with Walter Elliot (right) and Donald Gordon (left), the Chairman and Secretary respectively of the Trimontium Trust.

This helmet, in the Trimontium Trust exhibition in Melrose, is a replica of the famous brass helmet excavated by James Curle just before the First World War. The original is in Edinburgh.

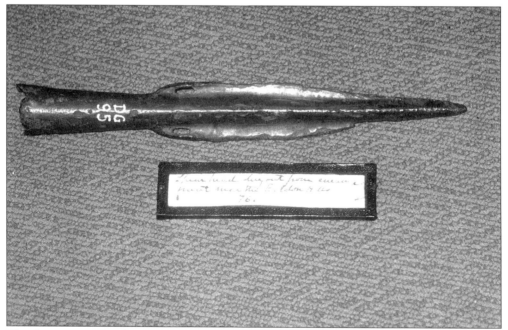

This Roman spearhead was found at Cauldshiels Loch, near Melrose, and is now in Edinburgh. The handwriting on the label is that of Sir Walter Scott.

Original Masonic Hall.

This pen-and-ink sketch of the original Newstead Masonic Hall was drawn by Mrs Drummond, the mother of Revd J. S. Drummond who composed the Melrose song. It was copied from Heatlie's drawing before he and Scott finished the painting.

William Heatlie died in 1892 before he was able to complete this painting of the Masonic hall, which was finished by Tom Scott. Notice the human touch that Scott added in the shape of the old man and his dog.

William Heatlie was born in 1848 at Ettrickbridgend. After living at Eildon Hall and Cloister Cottage – and after the death of his mother – Heatlie moved to St John's Cottage in St John's Wynd with his sister Isabella. There, when he wasn't teaching, Heatlie produced most of his paintings – watercolours of Borders scenes. He died in 1892 of influenza, aged forty-four.

Heatlie is buried with his sister Isabella in the Huntly Road cemetery.

This is the seal and matrix of Melrose Lodge, Number One *bis*, designed in 1788 by Brother John Smith of Darnick. Melrose Lodge shares the claim to be the oldest lodge in Scotland with St Mary's Lodge, Edinburgh.

A six-foot-long section of wall, marked with a plaque, is all that remains of the Newstead Masonic Hall.

The village of Newstead, photographed here from the North Eildon, claims to be the earliest continually inhabited village in Scotland, with a history going back two thousand years. The old railway line can be seen in front, now replaced by a bypass road.

Sadly, Newstead mill no longer exists. Only the millhouse remains, still occupied but much altered.

This picture of the mill was painted by George McDonald in 1944.

This is a view of Newstead village's main street, looking east.

This drawing is of the main street around the turn of the century.

The first cottage on the right of the two men, in another view of Newstead's main street, no longer exists.

This photograph of Admiral Sir Henry Fairfax KCB (1837-1900) of Ravenswood, in Newstead Village Hall, was taken by his wife. Sir Henry and Lady Fairfax were great benefactors, gifting a mission hall, a reading room and a library to the village. In his will Sir Henry also left money for a piped water supply.

## Eleven
# Bridges over the Tweed

*After the disappearance of the Roman bridge, which carried Dere Street across the Tweed (it is still not known exactly where this bridge was), the river was crossed from Melrose by ford and ferry. Today there are a number of bridges in use. At Leaderfoot there are three bridges: a modern road bridge, an old road bridge (now for pedestrians and cyclists only) and a disused railway viaduct. There are two other pedestrian bridges: the chain bridge between Melrose and Gattonside and the old railway bridge between Tweedbank and Galashiels. There was also one other bridge across the Tweed near Lowood House. It has long disappeared and it is uncertain what exactly it was like as only fanciful paintings of it remain today. The River Tweed is famous for its fishing. In season salmon and trout are plentiful.*

This is a drawing of the now completely vanished sixteenth-century bridge that used to cross the River Tweed near the present Lowood House, seen on the right of the bridge. The bridge was unusual in its design, having a central tower with drawbridges on either side. All traces of the bridge have totally disappeared. Here, the three Eildons are seen in the background.

This bridge over the Tweed at Lowood is sometimes referred to as 'Melrose Bridge' or the 'Bottle Bridge'. There was a bottle built in under the coping stone of the downstream parapet at the south end. However, it seems to have been removed during the recent refurbishment. This view of the bridge dates from 1992. A much earlier view is shown opposite.

374                                        MELROSE BRIDGE.

Lowood Bridge was built in the 1790s and stands where there used to be a ferry. In 1735 there was a tragic loss of life when the boat capsized in high water. There is now one lane only for traffic across the bridge, controlled by traffic lights.

In 1826 the ford between Melrose and Gattonside was replaced by this chain bridge. The building of the bridge began in 1825. John Smith of Darnick carried out the construction work and built the two pillars. The design and metalwork were the responsibility of Messrs Redpath, Brown and Co. There was a tollhouse at the south end to receive the portage. The bridge was opened in October 1826. The wooden roadway was $4\frac{1}{2}$ft wide and was suspended from chains by iron rods. It was notorious for swaying while people walked across.

In 1991 work began to strengthen and repair the chain bridge in accordance with European Union regulations. A third chain was added to each side to add strength to the support for the walkway. Also, as can be seen, each side received safety edging. The original tollhouse still stands at the south end of the bridge.

The viaduct, built in 1865 with nineteen tall, red, 13-metre-span, sandstone arches, carried the single-track railway line from Newtown St Boswells to Earlston and thence to Duns and Reston. The line was closed to passengers in 1948. The final closure came in 1966 when freight facilities were withdrawn. The viaduct was renovated and repaired recently and is waiting for further development. A steam engine can be seen pulling seven goods wagons and a guard's van from Earlston to Newtown in 1958.

The old road bridge at Drygrange was built by Alexander Stevens in 1779-1780 for the Turnpike Trust and has a 31-metre central span, exceptional for its date. Behind it is the modern bridge, built in 1971-1973 by Sir Alexander Gibb and Partners, which carries the A68 over the Tweed.

A 1920s view of Drygrange Bridge from the now-closed road from Newstead. Behind the bridge are the cottages of the small settlement that used to be found at the north end of the bridge.

Ashiestiel Bridge over the Tweed to the north-west of Selkirk was built by John and Thomas Smith of Darnick in 1848. Built of whinstone, this was, at the time of its construction, the longest (40-metre) single-span, arched, rubble bridge in the world.

On the Banks of the Tweed, Melrose.

A large, flat field on the banks of the Tweed is ploughed in 1913 by a two-horse plough. The size of the field and the straight furrows indicate the skill and industry of the ploughman. The background is possibly the eastern end of Gattonside Heights, with Kittyfield in the top left of the picture.

Here are two contrasting pictures of the River Tweed. This first one shows the river 'in spate' (flooded) at Lowood.

The second picture shows the Tweed at 'low water', at the site of the long-vanished bridge at Lowood (see p. 97).

# *Twelve*
# The Eildons

*Melrose itself is a little way back from the Tweed and tucked into the lower slopes of the Eildon Hills. There are three summits, but only two can be seen from the town, the North Eildon and the Mid Eildon, both 1,000ft above the market cross and about one mile away. The Eildons were well known to the Romans, hence Trimontium, which means 'Three Hills'. Moreover, the early Cistercian monks acquired building stone from the Eildons for their church. It has recently been realised that on Midwinter's Day at midday the shadow of the Mid Eildon is just about on the high altar of Melrose Abbey.*

This view of the hills is from the west. The Mid Eildon can be seen as the highest. Between the Mid and the West Eildons appears the Little Eildon. The three main Eildons are the remnants of long-extinct volcanic activity.

The North Eildon appears here on the Eildon Walk, now part of St Cuthbert's Way. This is the third stile on the walk to the summit.

The shape of the Eildon Hills shows clearly their volcanic origin. This winter view is from the east, from the village of Bemersyde, where Earl Haig resides in Bemersyde House.

The River Tweed is in the foreground. In the middle is Newstead, with Dean Road on the right. The North Eildon is covered in gorse bushes and peeping behind it on the right is the Mid Eildon, the highest of the three Eildons at 422 metres.

The houses in the foreground are in Darnick, those on the left in High Cross Avenue. The disused quarry is Quarry Hill, a volcanic outcrop, appearing on the right. To the right of Quarry Hill are houses in Douglas Road. Towering above is the North Eildon, the site of an Iron Age settlement.

In the foreground is Bowden Loch and to the right of the Mid Eildon can be seen the 'Baby Eildon'. Legend has it that King Arthur is buried somewhere here!

# Thirteen

# Peel Towers and Melrose Houses

*There are several peel towers around Melrose. Some are in ruins, one has totally vanished in Darnick and others have been renovated and are still occupied. They all display very thick exterior walls, evidence of the reason for their construction, which was protection against raiding parties. Apart from those in Darnick, the rest are in the countryside many miles to the north of Melrose. There are some interesting houses in and around Melrose, all privately owned except Harmony Hall, which now belongs to the National Trust for Scotland.*

This tower, dating from 1582, stands on the west side of Buckholm Hill, overlooking the Gala Water. It has only fairly recently become ruinous but still has interesting features. Little of the barmkin (defensive enclosure) survives but a stretch of the south wall shows a wide gateway with an arch. The tower has a main block of three storeys and an attic.

The Langshaw Tower and Allan (or Elwyn) walled garden, now largely wild, are pictured here. The third of the towers in the valley, it stands in a watercourse. The western and earliest part dates from the late sixteenth century. The original plan was L-shaped. Although it is now in ruins, the tower was occupied until the eighteenth century, when part of it was used as a school for the village of Langshaw Mill.

Hillslap Tower is L-shaped and has a lintel over the entrance dated 1585 that is flanked by the initials NC for Nicholas Cairncross and EL, his wife, who occupied the tower when it was known as Calfhill. It has recently been fully restored as a family home. To the right of the picture is Colmslie Tower.

Little is known of the early history of the Appletreeleaves peel tower. The first mention occurs in 1598 in 'Pitcairn's Criminal Trials', and the next in a valuation extract. Today it forms part of the clubhouse of Ladhope Golf Club, Galashiels.

This is from a sketch by James Skene (*c*. 1829). The Colmslie Tower is one of three towers within some 600 yards of each other in this valley, one of which, Hillslap, appears in the distance. Standing at the end of the Colmslie farmstead, the tower is oblong in plan and was at least three storeys high. Its lintel, with an armorial panel, is preserved over the farmhouse door and may date from soon after 1594. However, a sundial below the lintel, bearing the initials JM, is not older than eighteenth-century.

A fanciful sketch of Darnick Tower by the artist James Skene. (For more details on Darnick Tower, see pp. 71-72.)

This watercolour of Priory Farm and cottage, beside Melrose Abbey, was painted by William Heatlie in 1887.

In contrast, this is a photograph of the same farm and cottage in 1989.

Leslie House at the West Port, Melrose, was built in 1635. It received its name from being the house that was slept in by the Covenanter General David Leslie on the night before he defeated the royalist army of the Marquis of Montrose at Philiphaugh, Selkirk, on 13 September 1645. Leslie House was demolished in 1875.

Darnlee was a mini-mansion built by John Smith of Darnick for Dr Scott in 1817. In 1818 Dr Scott paid John Smith £200 and moved in. It was altered in 1872.

This mansion in red sandstone, with a balustraded balcony over an Ionic porch, was built in 1872.

Harmony Hall in Melrose, almost opposite the abbey, was built in 1807 by Robert Waugh, a Melrose carpenter who had made his fortune in Jamaica. He named his Melrose home after his Jamaican plantation. It now belongs to the National Trust for Scotland.

Originally a cottage called Burnfoot, Chiefswood was built by Sir Walter Scott in 1820 for his eldest daughter, Sophia, and son-in-law, biographer J.G. Lockhart. Part of Scott's novel *The Pirate* was written in the small room above the entrance.

## Fourteen
# Around Melrose

*Bowden village lies to the south of the Eildons and is clustered around a small village green. It has a fine historic church with a beautiful barrel-vaulted ceiling and a restored laird's loft. Newtown St Boswells lies to the east of the Eildons and was an important junction on the Waverley railway line. Earlston was the first station north of Newtown, across the Leaderfoot viaduct on the line to Reston. Thomas the Rhymer and Blaikie lived there. Blainslie is a tiny village north of Earlston on the old turnpike road from Jedburgh to Edinburgh. Dryburgh village, Hotel and Abbey are all on the east bank of the Tweed, near Bemersyde, the residence of Earl Haig.*

This view of Bowden Church is from the south. The church belonged to Kelso Abbey in 1180 but the oldest surviving part is the north wall which, with some restored barrel vaulting, dates from the fifteenth century. The rest of the building is mainly seventeenth-century or later. Some repairs were done in 1794 and it was fully restored in 1909.

The stairway seen in the previous picture leads to the chancel, originally separated from the church by a wall and used as a retiring room over the burial vault of the Dukes of Roxburghe. It has a finely moulded door, surmounted by this panel showing an earl's coronet and the respective crests of the Earl and Countess of Roxburghe. This is modern but the one below is dated 1644. The initials RER and ICR refer to Robert Ker, first Earl of Roxburghe and his countess, Jane Drummond.

This panel is above the entrance to the burial vault of the Riddell-Carre family and is dated 1611. The initials STK and DGH stand for Sir Thomas Ker and Dame Grisell Halkett, his wife. The laird's loft, which originally stood over the vault but within the church and which bears the same initials, has been moved and is still used by the family.

The seventeenth-century belfry contains this bell inscribed '*Soli Deo Gloria John Meikel me fecit Edinburgh Anno 1690*' ('Glory to God alone, John Meikel made me at Edinburgh in the year 1690'). A sundial dated 1660 is built into the south-west angle of the church.

This handsome gate bears the coronet and 'R' of the Roxburghe family. Alongside there is a mounting block, a reminder of the days when motor transport didn't exist.

In 1861 water was first channelled to this building from gravity on Bowden Common, to be held in a tank inside it, from which villagers drew it into pails. There was a cup for drinking water and a trough for animals.

Bowden is one of several Borders villages with a green – this is the south side of it. At the east end of the green, across from the pump, stands the war memorial. It was adapted from the old Mercat cross that dates from the late sixteenth century when Bowden obtained the privilege of holding a market, the first non-burghal one licensed in Scotland.

A view of the north side of Bowden village green.

The Roxburgh District Asylum became Dingleton Hospital in 1900, and was world-famous for its pioneering treatment of the mentally ill. Now the hospital is about to be closed and the future of the buildings is uncertain.

James Blaikie was an eighteenth-century wright. He was an excellent workman, deeply religious and a little eccentric. Many years before his death, he dug his grave beside his cottage and knelt daily in it to say his prayers. He also made a coffin and this gravestone which marks his burial place. His wife and daughter were buried close by.

Thomas the Rhymer returned from fairyland to Ercildoune (Earlston), where the ruins of his tower still remain. He became famous for prophecies, usually foretelling disaster. When a hart and a hind appeared in the village he took this as a summons from the Fairy Queen and disappeared with them for good. He was a real person, Thomas Learmont of Ercildoune who lived from around 1220 to around 1297, and was popularized in Sir Walter Scott's *Border Minstrelsy*.

This stone, at the top of the Bogle Burn road between Melrose and Eildon Village, marks the reputed site of the Eildon Tree. Legend says Thomas the Rhymer was carried off from this place by the Queen of the Fairies into the heart of the Eildon Hills for either three or seven years. An earlier stone on the other side of the road became lost in vegetation and this one was erected in 1929 then moved across the road in 1970. The whole setting has recently been redesigned.

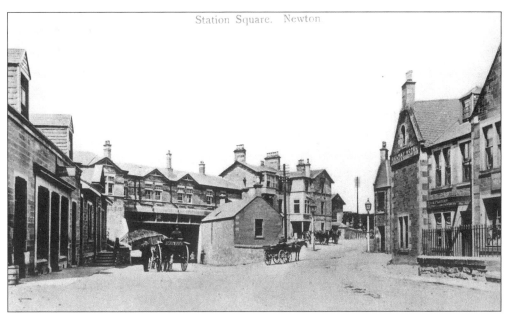

Station Square in Newtown St Boswells in the early twentieth century. There were two auction marts in the village at that time and the railways still carried stock, so the station was a busy place. However, after the closure of the railway line in 1969 the station was demolished and all the buildings in the centre of the photograph have gone. The Royal Bank of Scotland now occupies the building on the left and the Railway Hotel continues on the right.

The Black Hill lies between Drygrange and Earlston. Newstead Village lies to the west of the three large fields that cover the site of the Roman camp at Trimontium. Beyond the fields are the railway viaduct and the Drygrange road bridge.

Blainslie is a small village near Lander, ten miles north of Melrose. Before the days of motor transport, the blacksmith's work was essential to keep things moving. The smithy was also a popular meeting place in any community, as can be seen from this 1900 photograph.

In 1832 Sir Walter Scott was buried in Dryburgh Abbey. During the funeral procession from Abbotsford to Dryburgh, the horses pulling the coffin stopped at 'Scott's View' (see p. 9) for several minutes, refusing to move. The point at which they stopped was where Scott himself used to pause on his Border rides to admire the view of the Tweed valley and the Eildons. Here is Sir Walter's tomb, seen from the south-west.

This is the gate into the orchard, which is now treeless. The gate was erected by the Earl of Buchan and bears an inscription in honour of his parents: SATUM PARENTIBUS SUIS OPTIMIS SAC. D.S. BUCHANIAE. It translates as, 'This orchard was planted by his own hand by the Earl of Buchan, sacred to his parents who were the best'.

This statue of William Wallace was erected in 1814 by John Smith, the builder at Darnick, on the instructions of the Earl of Buchan. Sir Walter Scott did not like it at all and referred to it as a 'horrible monster'. The statue was renovated and repaired in 1991, as can be seen from the blade of the sword. A local newspaper reported on 1 April 1999 that this statue had been removed to Edinburgh to be displayed at the opening of the Scottish Parliament!